Teen Prayers by Teens

TEEN PRAYERS
by teens

Compiled by
Judith H. Cozzens

Pauline
BOOKS & MEDIA
Boston

Nihil Obstat:
  Reverend Thomas W. Buckley
Imprimatur:
  ✠ Most Rev. Seán O'Malley, O.F.M. Cap.
  Archbishop of Boston
  February 11, 2005

Library of Congress Cataloging-in-Publication Data

Teen prayers— by teens / compiled by Judith H. Cozzens.
   p. cm.
  ISBN 0-8198-7414-0 (pbk.)
  1. Catholic teenagers—Prayer-books and devotions—English. 2. Catholic Church—Prayer-books and devotions—English. I. Cozzens, Judith H.

  BX2150.T44 2005
  242'.83—dc22

                          2005001482

The Scripture quotations contained herein are from the *New Revised Standard Version Bible: Catholic Edition,* copyright © 1989, 1993, Division of Christian Education of the National Council of the Churches of Christ in the United States of America. Used by permission. All rights reserved.

Cover photo by Inmagine
Cover design and layout by Rosana Usselmann

Published by Pauline Books & Media, 50 Saint Paul's Avenue, Boston, MA 02130-3491.

Printed in the U.S.A.

www.pauline.org

Pauline Books & Media is the publishing house of the Daughters of St. Paul, an international congregation of women religious serving the Church with the communications media.

  3 4 5 6 7 8 9   11 10 09 08

*This book is dedicated to the young men and women
who serve the Catholic youth across our nation through
NET Ministries. Their dedication to prayer has
inspired me to collect these prayers, written by teens,
so that they can be shared with others.*

TABLE OF CONTENTS

Part I: Teen Prayers

Part II: Teen Prayers to the Saints

Part III: Teens' Favorite Traditional Prayers

WHAT IS NET MINISTRIES?

NET—National Evangelization Team Ministries—is a program that has responded to Pope John Paul II's challenge to "spread the Gospel." Based in St. Paul, Minnesota, NET offers youth evangelization training to volunteers aged eighteen to thirty. Forming teams of ten to twelve, these NET members share their faith during teen retreats from September to May, leading over a thousand retreats for approximately 70,000 teens each year. Drama, music, games, small group discussion, and large group presentations are all used to present basic Gospel messages in an exciting and dynamic way, and to invite every teen they meet to give their lives to the only One who can satisfy their hungry hearts—Jesus Christ.

But teens aren't the only ones changed by the NET experience. Serving on NET is a life-changing experience for the young adults, too. A volunteer's year of service with NET begins with a five-week training program. Team members receive instruction in prayer and Scripture, Catholic teachings, Christian character, content of the Gospel message, and ministry skills. The training course includes daily participation in the Eucharistic Celebration, Eucharistic Adoration, Reconciliation, time for reflection on the lives of the saints, individual and group prayer, and small group discussion. Participants are brought to a deeper understanding of their faith and given practical skills to effectively communicate that faith to others.

A year of service with NET gives the young volunteers the opportunity not only to share their faith with thousands of teens across the country, but also to have their own faith strengthened. This training and experience helps team members build a firm foundation for lives of service. After serving with NET, ninety percent of the participants continue in some form of service to the Church.

Some of the prayers in this book were written by the young adults who have served on NET, others by the young people who attended NET retreats, and still others by teens in youth groups and religious education classes. NET Ministries will receive all profits from the sale of this book and thanks the contributors for giving us permission to use their prayers for the benefit of the NET program.

For more information about NET MINISTRIES, please contact the NET office by emailing ministry@netusa.org or calling 651-450-6833.

HINTS FOR PRAYER

The Catholic tradition offers many ways to pray, and this prayer book offers three types of prayers that you might find appealing. The first section contains original prayers written by teens that bring everyday life to the Lord, and that acknowledge God's care about even the most ordinary events, such as friends, sports, and school. The second section taps into the tradition of praying for the saints' intercession for our needs, and introduces each saint with a brief biography. The third section offers a selection of some of the Church's traditional prayers with a teen's reflections on the importance of this prayer in his or her life.

Prayer is important in developing a relationship with Jesus Christ. It's like talking to a friend, listening, speaking, and being with that person. Learning to do this with God—sharing your innermost thoughts and feelings with him—can help you feel close to the Lord. Prayer can take many forms, like a simple conversation or a poem of praise. As Catholics, we are blessed to have both prayers that we pray together, like the Mass, and personal prayers like the ones found here.

Even if you have never really prayed before, take the first step now. If you keep trying, it will probably get easier. Practice will help you learn to pray. Soon you will be praying from the heart and truly sharing yourself with the Lord.

Some teens who submitted prayers for this book also submitted ideas on improving prayer times. Here are a few ideas to consider.

- I find that if I don't have a set prayer time each day, I forget to pray. Now I try to keep my appointment with God. — *Carrie*

- I get up and pray the first thing in the morning because it makes my whole day more fruitful. I find I have a better attitude when I start my day with prayer. — *Catherine*

- When I have a special place to pray, it helps me really talk to God. I pray in the corner of my bedroom. — *Edward*

- I like to look at something when I pray. I find that when I focus on an icon, a holy picture, or a sacramental—a religious object such as a crucifix—it helps me concentrate. — *Chris*

- I often use a Bible or a prayer book. Maybe this prayer book will help you improve your conversations with Jesus Christ! — *Jessica*

- When I find I am having trouble concentrating during my prayer time, I try new ways to pray. I have discussed this with my youth leader and my youth group to get ideas to improve my prayer time. — *Rachel*

- I set my watch to go off right before lunch, and when it beeps, it reminds me to say a prayer! — *Emil*

- When I was having trouble praying, I developed a ritual to help me focus my complete attention on Jesus. I say the following prayer very slowly and very deliberately, as many times as I need to, until I feel that I am "in conversation" with Jesus. If this helps you, you might try writing your own "focus prayer."

  My Lord, my God, and my King, bless me and keep me.
  Help me to know you, to see you, and to be yours.
  You are precious, you are holy, and you are worthy.
  My Lord, my God, and my King, bless me and keep me.

  — *Ed*

There are many ways to make a daily prayer time a part of your life. One format that might help improve your daily prayer is called a "Thirty-Day Walk with Jesus." Of course, it is only the beginning to a deeper prayer life. Here is how to make your own thirty-day walk with Jesus:

- **Fix your eyes on Jesus**: Start your time of prayer by focusing on Jesus and asking him to speak to you during your prayer. Turn your life over to Jesus and ask him to work in your heart.

- **Thanksgiving**: Spend time thanking God for the blessings you have received in your life.

- **Scripture**: Read the Scripture passage for the day listed on the next page. Ask yourself questions such as: "Who do I identify with in this Scripture passage?" "What does this passage say to me?"

- **Reflection and listening**: Ask yourself, "What is God saying to me through this Scripture? Is God using this passage to tell me something? Is God trying to ask me to do something?"

- **Intercession**: Tell God that you want to become closer to him, that you want to be more and more like Christ. Tell him about your needs and the needs of those you love.

- **Resolutions**: What do you want to do in response to what you have read and heard in this morning's prayer time? We suggest that you journal your resolution.

- Conclude with an "Our Father" and other prayers you like. These might include some of the prayers in our prayer book.

Scripture Readings for the Thirty-Day Walk with Jesus

Day 1	Luke 1:26-38	Hope
Day 2	Luke 2:1-20	Faith
Day 3	Luke 2:41-51	Confusion
Day 4	Matthew 3:13-17	Confirmation
Day 5	Matthew 4:1-11	Temptation
Day 6	John 1:35-51	Recognition
Day 7	John 2:1-12	Obedience
Day 8	Matthew 5:1-12	Instruction
Day 9	Mark 6:30-44	Abundance
Day 10	John 6:35-41	Hunger
Day 11	Matthew 5:13-16	Sharing
Day 12	John 9:1-41	Healing
Day 13	Luke 5:17-26	Forgiveness
Day 14	John 11:1-44	Love
Day 15	Mark 10:17-22	Treasure
Day 16	Mark 12:28-34	Commitment
Day 17	Matthew 16:13-19	Authority
Day 18	John 12:12-19	Praise

WHY PRAY? A TEEN'S VIEW

For some teens, praying is not a form of communication with God, but rather an endless chore. For me, prayer used to be a flow of meaningless words spoken from habit. I just repeated the same words day after day, words that meant nothing to me, and this caused my whole faith in God to feel empty.

One day my religion teacher told us not to mindlessly mumble prayers, but to feel them and to take the words we are saying to heart. That day, I started praying with more attention—both traditional prayers and prayers of my own—and since then, my prayer life has matured and I feel a stronger, more personal bond with God. I never dreamed that a simple prayer that is recited by countless people every day could mean so much, or that I could deeply reflect on each and every word in one of my own prayers! When I pray this way, prayer is no longer an unpleasant task, but a way for me to talk to God and express my faith. I hope that everyone who uses this prayer book can find a stronger faith through prayer, just as I did.

— *Kathleen*

Remember

Prayer is our avenue to a relationship with God. God is available to us every moment of every day. Let's decide to make ourselves available to God.

"Draw near to God and God will draw near to you."

James 4:8

PART I:
TEEN PRAYERS

PART I: TEEN PRAYERS

Remember: God *wants* us to pray. God hears our prayers, and prayer can happen in so many ways. If you lose your keys and ask God to help you find them, *that's prayer*. When you see a beautiful sunset and say, "Thank you, Lord," *that's prayer*. As St. Thérèse of Lisieux told us, "…prayer is a surge of the heart; a simple look turned toward heaven, a cry of recognition and of love that embraces both trial and joy." In other words, anything at all can be turned into prayer!

As you read the prayers we've gathered, mark your favorites so you can find them easily. And feel free to change the words when you want to add your own thoughts. That way, when you read these poems and petitions, they'll become *your* prayers.

FAITH

Give Me Faith

Heavenly Father, I need you to survive my daily life! And so, I'm asking for a strong belief in you. I know that without you, I am nothing. Please help me to have faith in you, so that I can live my life with you at my side. Amen.

— *Anna*

Set Me Free

My God, my Savior,
I don't know how to love you.
My heart feels imprisoned by iron bars—

some of my own making; some that others have
    caused.
Selfishness and arrogance are often my jailers.
Lord, break me free!
Bring your love—your dynamite—
to blow apart the bars,

and your mercy to pick open the lock.
Let love burn this prison's walls,
break up the foundation stones,
and I, stepping forth from the rubble,
will learn to love you more.

— *Bernadette*

Help Me Believe

Lord, I know that you love me. I want to give you everything in response to your love, but something is holding me back and I can't figure out what it is. Give me the strength to follow you, no matter what. Help me believe in your love. Amen.

— John

Clarity

Lord, please grant me clarity. When I'm confused, please be with me. When I'm lost and unsure, squeeze my hand so I'll know you walk with me. When I have trouble walking, please carry me. Clear my vision so my eyes will be firmly fixed on you and remind me that you are always with me. Amen.

— Mary

Reassure Me, God

Today when I woke up, I wondered if you're real.
As I lay in bed, I kept asking, "Are you there,
    God?"
But you didn't answer.
I know you're supposed to be there,
but sometimes it would help if you'd let me know.
Help me to know you love me, Lord.
I just want reassurance. Amen.

—Jeff

Sincerity

Dear God, help me to become a better Christian. I go to Mass every weekend, but sometimes I don't pay attention. I say a prayer before I eat, but it's not always a prayer from my heart. I often forget to pray at night.

Help me to pray with meaning, so I can become closer to you. Help me to live in truth: honestly and without pretense. You are the light that will guide me, and I want to praise your name with all my heart as I follow your way!

— *Theo*

Help Me to Remember You

When I was tired last night
you just slipped my mind
because I had started the day
simply lagging behind.

I woke up today
and headed to school.
Then, I sat there at lunch
with a quick thought of you.

I figured I'd talk
with you later...sometime.
But then I had practice
and again you slipped my mind.

After some homework
and a quick bite to eat,
I felt so exhausted
I just wanted to sleep.

Thus ended a day
where I had forgotten about you,
and the cycle continues,
now what can I do?

Please remind me that you
must never be dismissed.
You are more than just
a "to-do" on my list.

I can remember you
in every event in my day.
It's really not hard,
just guide me that way.

With every action
big or small,
help me glorify your name,
Most Holy of all.

I love you, Lord!
Please help me always to tell you so.
Never let a day pass
without me making sure you know.

— Karen

Praying My Distractions

God, so often I find myself thinking about things during Mass: problems, worries, school, work, friends. I know I should probably be focusing on you, but maybe this is how I can bring my life to you. Please help me to offer everything to you, Lord. Allow me to realize and appreciate the beauty of the Mass and to turn everything—even my distractions—into prayer. Amen.

— *John*

Help Us, Lord

When the world seems lost… Help us, Lord.

When peace seems far away… Help us, Lord.

When disasters happen… Help us, Lord.

When we don't understand… Help us, Lord.

When we get mad at each other… Help us, Lord.

When we are sad… Help us, Lord.

When we are crying… Help us, Lord.

When love seems gone… Help us, Lord.

When we forget to pray… Help us, Lord.

When things don't go our way… Help us, Lord.

When our hearts are not open… Help us, Lord.

When we don't follow you… Help us, Lord.

— *Michael*

Prayer Before Jesus in the Eucharist

Good Jesus,
you drench me with your abundant love.
You fill me with your abundant joy.
You ask me to bring you my joys and sorrows,
happy times and sufferings,
so that I may be closer to you.
You wait for me patiently.
You shower me with your hope.
You direct my paths with wisdom.

Good Jesus,
help me to never forget that you are always
present in the Eucharist.
Remind me of your holy presence.
Strengthen my frail faith, so that I may never
abandon you
or deny you, Jesus.
Let me share your love, your joy, and your peace

with my brothers
and sisters.
Make me strong, O Lord.
Through your Sacrament of Love, give me the
grace to live well,
so that I may praise you throughout my life.
Amen.

— Ann

"God in the Sky"

In my preschool years, I heard
that God made me
and no matter how I goofed up
that God forgave me.

So I sat and I learned
about God on high.
In Sunday school I felt the love
of that "God in the sky."

In my grade school years I worried
that someday soon I'd be dead,
and God's love couldn't penetrate
the scared thoughts in my head.

So I cried and I thought
about how I could die.
I prayed I wouldn't go too soon
to that "God in the sky."

In my junior high years I wondered
if God might not be real
and I stopped trying to believe
in what I could not feel.

So I turned myself away
from God, not caring why
or how I had lost my belief
in that "God in the sky."

But now in high school I've found
that I don't really care
whether others think that God exists—
for I believe you're there.

So now I try to trust and pray
to you, God on high
and now I feel I'm loved for sure
because you are by my side.

— *Anne*

GOD'S PLAN FOR MY LIFE

Trust

Dear Lord, my life is full of so many questions and I don't know the answers.

Help me to look to you and to find the right way to go.

Help me to trust you and to know that the answers will come in time.

Help me not to worry and to become depressed, but to know you are there.

I ask this in your name. Amen.

— *John*

Prayer of Acceptance

Lord,
I have a burden to bear,
a thorn in my side.
I wish it weren't there,
but it is anyway.

Let me live faithfully,
despite my sufferings,
and feel your presence with me
whatever happens today.

— *Rob*

Vocation

Dear God,

Help me know what to do with my life.

I'm confused.

I want to live my life according to your will

and to serve you in whatever I do.

But there are so many choices.

Please help!

— *Drew*

Searching for God

Is there anybody out there listening to me?
Listening to my prayers, my thoughts, and my
    pleas?
God, if you are out there, answer, PLEASE!
I'm wanting you, begging you, down on my
    knees.

Is there anybody out there listening to me?
I can't deal with life alone, can't you see?
I need someone to be watching over me.
Someone to guide and protect me constantly.

Is there anybody out there listening to me?
Help me open the closed door. Where is the key
to open my eyes to God's purpose for me?
I want to be the person he wants me to be.
Please, God, help me to know you are listening
    to me.

— *Dan*

To Be More Like You

Jesus, present in my heart,
show me how to be more like you.
Help me to trust in your plan
and to do what you want me to;
let me always be a reflection of your love to
      others.

— *Mary*

Holy Spirit, Come!

Holy Spirit, come cleanse me of all that does not reflect you, and allow your grace to grow in me. Fill my heart with love and my mind with understanding. Help me to know the plan you have for me in this life and give me the courage to follow it.

Holy Spirit, come and renew my faith in Christ and lead me to him. Come show me the path of life and guide me always closer to you. Amen.

— *Megan*

To Be a Light

Father, help me to be good.
Help me shine like the sun
and draw others to your light.

— *Mark*

Following God's Way

Holy Spirit,
help me to be vigilant
in everything I do.
Help me to be just,
and never, ever untrue.
Help me through
all the hard times in the day,
even when I forget
to stop in and say, "Hey."
Remind me to follow your way. Amen.

— *Luke*

Choosing the Future

Lord, I've been putting it off, but I can't delay much longer. I have to make the important college decision. I'm excited and afraid, too. I want to go one minute and the next I want to stay right where I am. I don't know what you want me to do. Help me to choose well. Help me to find what I should do with my life. Give me the wisdom and strength to do the right thing. Amen.

— *Ann Marie*

GUIDANCE

Morning Prayer

Dear Lord,

take me through this day,

safe and in your presence.

Guide me when I encounter trouble or
uncertainty.

Let me be more patient with what I do not
understand,

and shepherd me in the ways of forgiveness.

Amen.

— *Aaron*

Carry me, Jesus

Come, Lord Jesus,
meet me in my brokenness and carry me.
Let me be the lamb upon your shoulders.
Teach me to hear your voice.
Come to me in my confusion and heal me.
You are my Lord and my King.
You are the Shepherd of my soul.

— *Tracy*

Help Me to See You

Holy God, help me to see
your true glory and your true beauty
wherever I look,

for you are all around me
and if I paid attention,
everything could be a sign pointing to you.

— *Adam*

To Follow Your Ways

Lord, help me to follow you
even when I'm angry and frustrated
and feeling alone.

—*Jeff*

Thanks for Guiding Me

Lord, at times I wonder how some live at all,
without a God, a hand to hold, someone to catch
their fall.
You carry me through hardships,
you are with me when I'm scared.
You will walk with me until the end,
and you answer every prayer.
Though I may not listen much,
you always know what's best:
the path to make, the road to take,
and when to stop for rest.
And I guess I'm trying to say
thank you for everything,
for every day and every breath.
To you every day praises I will sing.
You've blessed me with these many gifts.
Thank you, thank you, now and forever.
Thank you until the end. Amen.

— *Anastasia*

Struggling to Understand

Dear God, I don't know what's happening, but I need your help. I want to understand love, but all I can think about is sex. I don't want to be obsessed by it or afraid of it, but sometimes I feel like I'm both! Sex is supposed to be a gift for marriage, but I'm struggling to understand it *now*. I don't want to be immature about it, but I just don't know how to handle things: my feelings change, my attitudes change; I feel curious and then nervous and then guilty and then anxious. Please, God, just help me to live faithfully and with integrity, bringing my confusion to you with straightforward confidence in your all-powerful love for me. Guide me, Lord! Amen.

— *Juanita*

Protect Me, Lord

Beautiful Savior,

teach me the way of your love.

Let your mercy pour forth and wash me clean.

May I be humble in spirit and in deed.

May my heart and soul cry out to you, Lord.

May I seek refuge and find my strength by your
    side.

In your heart hold me,

by your side heal me,

renew me, and with your hands guide me. Amen.

— *Tracy*

FOLLOWING CHRIST

Jesus, My Savior

Urgent to get through to me,
he breaks down the walls,
consumes my heart.
Insistent, he whispers,
 "Today is the day, now the hour!
Give me your life."

— *Bernadette*

Prayer of Hope

My hands, my feet, and my breath: words and
     body,
my very life,
my soul, my heart, and my love,
these I surrender.
Should my path grow dark, the night long, the
     terrors close,
should my heart be shattered, my mind lost, my
     very body torn,
I vow, I choose, I know,
I will follow
you, my glorious Lord, God and King.
To your invitation, I cry out, YES!
And I live
for you.

— Ed

Jesus Your Friend: A Rap Poem

When life gets tough, you have a friend.
He'll be there for you until the very end.
If you're feeling blue and life seems too hard to
        bear,
just call for him and he'll be there.
He's the one who makes the sun rise and the
        flowers grow,
he's the one who puts the sparkle in the falling
        snow.

Who is this great one, you ask?
His name is Jesus Christ, the Savior.
Let me tell you what he has done for us.

He lived, died, and rose to set us free,
so that with God we could forever be.
So when you're feeling down and don't know
        where to go

know that you'll never be alone.

Remember that when you are with Jesus, you
    have a friend.

One that will be there until the very end.

— Megan

Keep Calling Me

Good Shepherd, I hear your voice call me
but I cannot see you.
I want to see you,
I want to follow,
I just can't right now;
there are these things in my life that you won't
    like.

Your voice is still calling;
gentle and sweet are your words.
Lord, don't you understand?
You don't want me;
you must want someone else,
someone who has it all together.

Louder I hear your voice
still inviting me,
asking me to leave these things behind.
But what if I can't, Lord?
What's that, Lord?

Trust you?
Follow you?
I want to, Lord, but I don't think I can do it
    on my own
I just can't.

"My child,
I will help you if you let me,
give these things over to me,
you have had them for way too long.
Hear my voice,
see my face,
trust and follow me;
I will not abandon you.
Will you follow me?"

Good Shepherd,
I will follow wherever you lead.
Help me to give these things over to you
and to trust in your words.
I love you. Amen.

— *Tracy*

Following the Narrow Way

Dear God,

Sometimes I feel like you are calling me.

I can almost see you beckoning me to come and follow you.

To be honest, I'm not sure I want to, Lord.

I don't know if I can give my life to you.

How can I leave behind everything I've known?

Lord, if you're really calling me to serve on your behalf, show me.

Give me the strength to hear your voice and to follow your plan for me. Amen.

— *Chris*

The Sacrifice for Me

Lord.

I cannot imagine what you went through—for
    me.

Everything sacrificed.

I look upon your face, bloodied and bruised.

I can't even imagine that you could love me
    this much:

Cross across your broken back,

nails through your hands and feet,

blood running down your face.

It was sin that cost your life,

and your unwillingness to back down from truth.

Your life, given all for me...for us.

I want to do nothing but offer you all my days.

To live my life as one of your disciples,

saying, "Thank you, my Lord." Amen.

— *Patrick*

I Will Follow You

Lost, confused, in a world of lies
tripping, falling, blinded eyes,
where am I?
Am I really here?
What's the plan?
Please make it clear.
Lead me, guide me
through the dark and unknown,
take me, show me,
I don't know where to go.
Teach me, tell me
what it is you want of me, for
I am ready.
Just point out where you want me to go
I will follow
you.
In my head there is a voice
telling me to make a wrong choice,

saying that it is okay,
but I don't want to live that way.
Lead me, guide me
through the dark and unknown,
Take me, show me,
I don't know where to go.
Teach me, tell me
what it is you want of me, for
I am ready.
Just point out where you want me to go
I will follow
you.

— *Muffin*

KINDNESS

A New Heart

Dear Savior, I pray to you asking for a loving heart. Please help me to find the good in everyone and everything I encounter. Teach me to be more like you, to treat others with love and respect. Today, I judged someone and said hurtful things about her. Tomorrow, give me the strength to do what is right. Amen.

— *Anna*

Teasing Others

Lord, please forgive me for making fun of others. Sometimes I feel so insecure with myself that I find things wrong with everyone else, just to make myself feel better. After gossiping about someone, I feel better for a while, but then I feel guilty about it. Sometimes I make fun of somebody without noticing what I'm doing. It's a bad habit, and I know it's wrong. Help me not to get wrapped up in the moment when I'm the center of attention, feeling popular and cool, and make the wrong decision. I want to start following you more closely; I need to start treating others as I would like to be treated. Please forgive me for making fun of others and help me to be strong enough to resist this temptation. Amen.

— Anna

Loneliness

Dear God, there's a kid at school who is always alone. He doesn't eat with anyone, doesn't meet anyone between classes, doesn't look at anyone. I've said something to him a few times, but he doesn't really answer. It's like he doesn't want friends. He must be really lonely. Should I tell someone, a teacher or coach maybe?

Lord, I've been lonely, too, and I know how much it hurts. If you were in my place, Lord, you'd find a way to be his friend. Guide me to find a way to be a Good Samaritan, Lord, and to lighten his load if I can. Amen.

— *Jack*

Smiles

Dear Lord,
I praise you for creating smiles.
A smile is something anyone can do.
Smiles brighten up people's days
and tell others how much we like them.
The simple gesture of a smile
can cause a chain reaction of happiness.
Thank you for all the goodness that smiles cause.
Please remind everyone to smile
and make someone's day a little happier.
— *Camilla*

Jealousy

Lord God, help me to recognize the goodness you've placed within me. Sometimes I'm tempted to look at the talents and good things that others have, and to feel small and insignificant beside them. But I have a lot to be grateful for, and I know you've given me gifts to share. When the jealousy monster threatens to take over, help me to be happy for the many different ways you are praised by others' talents. And help me to share one of my gifts with someone else today. Thank you, Lord.

— *Tammy*

HONESTY/INTEGRITY

Self Identity

God, let me know myself, and give me the peace this brings. You've created me in your image—help me as I struggle to find my identity. Let me see *you* in me and love you—*in me!* Amen.

— *Joe*

Truth

Jesus, please help me to always speak with honesty. Help me to have the courage to tell the truth, even when it would be easier to lie. I know I sometimes hurt others with my words. Let me learn honesty and kindness, Lord, and teach me to think before I speak. Amen.

— *Anna*

Making Media Choices

God,
what I hear and what I see
affects what I do, and who I am,
and how I see others.
Sometimes, music turns my thoughts and
        actions toward drugs and drinking.
Sometimes, images I see make me think that in
        order to be cool,
I must fit into the mold that the media place
        in front of me.
When I dwell on messages that disrespect
        people,
I can no longer see your light.
Help me to find music that builds up
instead of tearing down.
Help me to change channels when a show
        comes on
that I know I shouldn't watch.

Make me your messenger:

help me talk to my friends about what we

watch and listen to.

Together, we can find beauty in the world.

There is no need to hide behind pictures and
    words

that keep us from being our very best selves.

— Jan

Truthfulness

Lord, I need your help. I keep lying, but I don't want to. Help me to tell the truth no matter how hard it may be. I know you're there for me, telling me what I should do. I just have to listen.

— *Rob*

Keeping Promises

Lord, a person's word is supposed to be true. Help me to reflect your truth in all I do and say. It's easy to say one thing and to mean another, especially if I'm trying to avoid responsibility. But you want integrity from your followers: "Say 'yes' when you mean 'yes' and 'no' when you mean 'no.'" Help me to keep my promises and to be more responsible so that others can count on me. Amen.

— *Steve*

SCHOOL

A Prayer Before a Test

Holy Spirit, please guide me. Help me to remember what I've studied for this exam. Take all of my anxiety away and give me a clear and focused mind; don't let me panic! I've done all that I can to prepare myself, so just be with me and get me through it. Amen.

— *Carrie*

Doing Your Best

Lord, between homework, sports, band, and helping around the house, I've got so many deadlines to meet. Help me!

I need a good attitude, even when everything seems to happen at once and there's just not enough time for it all. Help me!

I really want to be a good sport when things don't go my way and to accept what I have done when it is my best. Help me!

I want to be honest and not cheat, even if it means I get a lower grade. Help me!

And let me remember that a test at school is not nearly as important as doing what is right and good.

Lord, help me just to do my best in everything, and let all that I do praise you. Amen.

— *Annie*

Too Much Homework!

God, don't teachers know that their class isn't the only one? I have so much homework tonight I don't know how I'm going to do it all. There are books everywhere—my room looks like the library.

I want to do well, but I feel a lot of pressure right now. And when I'm stressed-out, it's hard to focus. My parents want good grades, I just want to pass.

Be with me, God. Help me to get through this night!

— *Kip*

In the Zone

When I'm running well and in the zone,
it's like nothing can touch me.
I'm fast and free
and all the problems that were so heavy before
blur as I race past.

Running on an autumn afternoon
with the rest of the team,
I feel part of it all,
a member of the "human race,"
ready to take on the world.

I praise you, God, for this incredible feeling.
It's like there's nothing else I need to do
but run
for you.

— *Brandon*

Endings and Beginnings

The year will soon be coming to an end,
and I can feel the changes coming already.
Tears of joy at graduation,
tears of sadness, too.
And the feeling of uncertainty
about the years ahead.

Fear of losing memories,
fear of drifting apart,
fear of being lost in a new life.
The year will soon be coming to an end,
and now each day counts!

I want to take time to
make memories that will last forever.
I'm not ready to leave behind
these years of my life:
friends,
school,
sports,
and everything.
Soon there will be a new beginning.
Lord, help me to remember my past and be
excited about my future. Amen.

— *Michael*

FRIENDS

Prayer for Friends

May God watch us while we're parted.

May God bless you when you're downhearted.

May God keep you safely in his arms.

Even when you're sad or afraid,

he'll be there to help you make it.

All of this and more is what I pray

for you

forever and ever. Amen.

— *Laura*

For Friends with Problems

Jesus, you have blessed me so richly with a loving family. Your abundant love has showered me with so many gifts that I often fail to even notice them.

In your kindness and mercy, Lord Jesus, please bless each and every person I love who carries a burden—a cross—that seems really heavy:

Help my friends who are coping with their parents' divorce.

Be with the kids who walk the same halls as I do each day, wondering if they will have food on their table at night.

Embrace anyone who doesn't feel your love, Lord. Please help me to never again take for granted the many blessings you've given me. Amen.

— *Sarah*

Prayer of a Concerned Friend

Most Holy Father,
my dearest friend has slipped away,
alcohol has taken over his life.
Give me the strength to face him.
I need your guidance,
he needs your help.
Put your words in my mouth,
put your fire in my spirit,
put your love in my actions,
for without you I am nothing,
but with your help, I can do anything.
Lord, I would do anything for this friend,
help me reach out to him
with courageous love. Amen.

— *Jan*

A Prayer for My Friends

Lord,
I ask you to protect my friends.
Sometimes they drink or use drugs.
Please don't allow alcohol or drugs to catch them in the addiction trap.

Please also strengthen my resolve to choose not to drink or do drugs with them or with anyone else.
And, finally, help me to accept that in most cases my prayers and my own decision to be strong may be all that I can do to help my friends.

— *Rob*

After the Game

Dear Lord, thanks for letting me have such a good time last night. It's fun being with a bunch of classmates, cheering for the team and just hanging out. Thanks for giving me such great friends, too. I feel like I can talk to them about anything—serious stuff and "whatever stuff"—and they'll be there for me when I need them. I'll be there for them, too, because that's what friends are for. Thanks for getting us home safely and for being able to look forward to next weekend's game!

— *Zach*

PRAISE

To the Father

Father,
you are amazing.
You are great.
You are loving.
You understand.
You forgive.
You created our lives
and gave us freedom.
There is nothing you cannot do.
I give you praise. Amen.

— *Sam*

Who Do You Say That I Am?

Jesus, you are so many things to me.
You are my Rescuer:
Before you came, I was lost.
Now I will never be lost again.

You are my Shelter:
Near you I am safe.
Resting against your heart, pressing my cheek
to your feet, your hands, your ravaged side,
when I am with you,
I feel like nothing else can touch me.

You are my Strength:
I say, "Jesus," and the grace comes.
The impossible becomes easy—
or at least bearable!

You are my Master:
You stand before me beckoning to me,
pointing out to me the way that I should go,
refusing to be put off by my whining and weak-
ness.

You are my Creator,
who delights to see me smile,
who dotes on my every word,
who laughs to see me dance,
who calls me a masterpiece.

You are the one watching over me,
providing for my every need.
You will not let my life perish unfulfilled.
You are my King, Friend, and Master.
My Jesus, you are everything.

— *Bernadette*

Saving Us

Jesus, I praise you for coming to this world and for living with such integrity. You were so amazing and brave to die on the cross. Your suffering showed us how much you love us—you were willing to sacrifice your life for us. Lord, help me to do whatever I can to help others and spread God's word.

— *Nicole*

A Spotlight

Lord, I want to be a huge spotlight,
shining full on you,
so the world will see you,
even in the dark of night,
and believe.

— *Bernadette*

Stars

O Lord, each star in the night sky reminds me of your love and glory. When I walk down the wrong path, your love is like those stars, little specks of light in the dark, leading me toward you. When I look into the sky and see all of the stars, I think about your grace and beauty. The beautiful stars reflect your glory, and when I see them, I am thankful.

— *Brianna*

Life

Life is a wonderful thing. Thank you for creating me. Help me to live my life to the fullest. Life is beautiful, life is wonderful, and life is fulfilling. Life is so much more than a series of events. Help me to recall the many good times in my life and give you thanks. I praise you for giving me the gift of life, in this world and the next. Amen.

— *Tom*

Seeking Jesus

Jesus, there are days
when I don't seem to know you very well,
nor do I always recognize your face.
But sometimes—from time to time—
I hear an echo of your voice
in my hesitant ears,
compelling and irresistible.
My heart jumps up!
I rush to find you
and catch the wake of your passing.
You are the one my heart loves,
you are the one I long for.
Let me find you every day! Amen.

— *Bernadette*

LIVING FOR OTHERS

Christ in My Day

Sometimes in the morning, I take a lot of time getting ready for the day. I worry about my hair and what I will wear, but I forget to take time to prepare my heart for encountering you during the day.

Lord, please place kindness in my heart for those I meet. Put generosity in my heart for those in need. Prepare to reach out through me to those in pain. Help me to worry less about how I look. Place your light in my heart so that others will see you in me. Amen.

— *Ann Marie*

Those in Need

Lord, I am sorry for ignoring the cries of those in need. Please help me to find more time and energy to give to others. Amen.

— *Bobby*

The Poor and the Suffering

Lord, please help our brothers and sisters who are hungry or suffering. Comfort them with your love and relieve their suffering with your mercy. Lord, every time I see or think about these sick and suffering people, I'm sad, knowing that I do so little to help. Help me to do more. Help me to provide food for the food drives, donate money to help those in need, and to volunteer at shelters when I can. One day on earth, may there be no more suffering, no more hunger, and no more sickness. Amen.

— *Matt*

Giving My Gifts

God, please forgive me when I am not thankful for the gifts that I receive. Help me to remember those who do not have all the things I have, and let me help them by passing on some of the blessings I have received.

— *Christopher*

Showing Love

It is amazing
what a little love can do,
a spoonful of attention
when you are feeling kind of blue.

It only takes a bear hug
to show I care,
or a voice that says hello,
and a smile that says I love you so.

It only takes a sharing word
that says I understand,
a call that says I thought of you,
or an outstretched hand.

I thank you, God, for all of this
for your love is what makes us
respond to a hug, a smile, or a caring way—
the little things that show you are with us today.

— *Derek*

Giving to Others

Lord, many people in this world suffer more than I do. Forgive me for not being as generous as I should and for not using my abilities to help others in need. I know that there are many opportunities all around me to give to others. Help me, Lord, to use my talents and my resources in a way that would honor you and make a difference. Amen.

— *Alex*

PEACE

Give Us Peace

Keep us at peace and protect us from violence.
Keep us from doing and thinking evil.
Please help all who suffer from war, lost loved
ones, and hunger.
Bring us peace, O Lord. Amen.

— *Michael*

Times of Difficulty

Dear God,
help me to see the good in the bad times,
help me to feel your presence in the sad times,
and when I'm in distress,
wipe away the tears from my eyes. Amen.

— *Tammy*

Fighting Depression

My Savior, please lift the darkness from my heart and show me your light. Help me not to put too much pressure on myself and to seek assistance from my family and friends when I need it. Allow me to find pleasure and contentment in my life. Help me see the good in others and in myself.

Let happiness brighten my heart, mind, and soul once again. Amen.

— *Rachel*

When I Am Weary

Grant me joy when I'm in pain,
grant me peace when I'm distraught.
Give me laughter when I am happy,
and love when I am not.
Grant me light when I'm in darkness,
grant me hope when I'm in doubt.

Give me a spark of strength when I'm weary,
and the will not to blow it out.
Grant me the patience to forgive,
grant me the courage to let go.
Give me the strength to overcome,
and the willingness to let it show.
Grant me wisdom through my failure,
grant me understanding through my mistakes.
Give me guidance and endurance,
in whatever path I take.
Grant me faith when I struggle,
grant me safety when I fall.
Give me the want to keep on living,
and love through it all. Amen.

— *Catherine*

It Feels So Wrong

Why, Lord?

Why are the ones I love gone while I'm still here?
I know that they would want me to live on, but
still, Lord, it feels so wrong.

Help me to keep living and to find joy again,
and to do some good in honor of my loved ones
who are gone.

Please help me to follow you one day at a time.

— *Jan*

Help Me to Hang On

Right now, life just doesn't feel worth living. And yet I know you want me to go on.

Lord, you have to help me see the way. I feel darkness pressing in all around me and I need your light.

Lord, help me to find the way out. Help me to know you are there. Please send someone to reach out a hand to show me that you are with me. Amen.

— *Paul*

From Myself, Save Me

My mind is full of much confusion,
chaos is making its intrusion,
I've lost myself in introversion.
God help me,
is this all illusion?
I love you,
you love me.
I think that's true, but I don't know *me*.
My thoughts are too many.
I have lost control; can you save me?
Take me, Lord. From myself save me.

I'm overwhelmed with situations,
remove this extra information,
make room for your visitation,
Creator, make new your creation.
God help me,
is this all illusion?

I love you,
you love me.
I think that's true, but I don't know *me*.
My thoughts are too many.
I have lost control; can you save me?
Take me, Lord. From myself save me.

— *Muffin*

Justice in the World

God,
things are out of balance in the world.
Some people have lots
and others don't have enough.
Some countries are so powerful
and others can't get the help they need.
Some people are hungry and sick
and others waste food and throw away clothes
when they get tired of them.

God,
inspire governments and world leaders
to realize that power and money aren't the most
important things,
and to work to eliminate hunger, unemployment,
and disease.

God,
grant us the desire to understand other cultures
and give us peace in our day. Amen.

— *Liz*

FORGIVENESS

Forgive Me

Dear Lord,
Please cleanse me of my sins.
Please forgive me for the wrong things
I have done and the right things I have failed to
    do.
Forgive me for not always respecting others
and doing what I know is good.
Please forgive me for failing to be
understanding and forgiving
to everyone around me.
With your mercy
I will strive to become a better person.
I will forgive anyone who has hurt me in any
    way,
so they, too, will know the blessing of forgive-
    ness. Amen.

— *Camilla*

The Ten Commandments

Lord, you gave us these ten laws so that we would know how you want us to live our lives here on earth. Forgive us when we fail.

Forgive us when we do not honor and love you above all things.

Forgive us when we take your name in vain.

Forgive us when we don't make Sunday your special day.

Forgive us when we dishonor our parents or guardians.

Forgive us when we strike out at others in anger or revenge.

Forgive us when we treat others as objects for our fun and pleasure.

Forgive us when we take and steal from others.

Forgive us when we lie to our friends or parents.

Forgive us when we stubbornly fantasize about others.

Forgive us when we covet our neighbors' belong-
    ings.

Lord, help me to follow the Ten Command-
ments, avoiding temptation and sin, and living
my life to the fullest. Amen.

— *Matt*

Help Me Put You First

My God, I need your forgiveness. Sometimes I do the wrong thing even though I know the right thing; and I know you wouldn't approve of my choice. I feel bad when I ditch Mass on Sunday to do something that I think is more fun. Lord, please help me to push away those things that take me away from you. Help me make time to go to church and to pray.

And I'm sorry for not praying and talking to you on my own even when I know that I should. Help me to put you first in my life, dear Lord, today and every day. Amen.

— *Annie*

Act of Contrition

God, I'm truly sorry that I have sinned against you time after time. You have been so good to me and still I choose things that are wrong. Please help me to resist temptation and evil in the future. God, I humbly ask you for forgiveness for all my sins. Please give me your blessing this day. In Jesus' name, I pray. Amen.

— *Brianna*

Help Me to Trust You

Dear Lord, please forgive me for not always following your teachings. When I take your name in vain, gossip, put people down, and whine about having to go to church, remind me that in order to be like you, I have to avoid sin. I'm sorry for not always having a strong faith in you. Please help me to learn to trust you more. When I'm in a situation that I don't know how to handle, help me to stop and think what you would do, so that I will do what is right. Amen.

— Jan

Swearing

Dear Father, help me follow your commandment and not take your name in vain. And please forgive me for swearing, too. Help me to control my temper and to stop this bad habit, because swearing is hurtful and I swear *way* too much.

— *John*

Forgive Them, Forgive Me

When Jesus was beaten,
and handed the cross,
it hurt him
in more ways than one.
He fell when he carried the cross,
and struggled to endure the pain,
but he still went on. He said:

"Forgive them, Father,
for they know not what they do."
Some people do not realize
that God's love is real and true.
We need to know this
and believe that God's love is true.

When Stephen was stoned, he did not run away.
He stood his ground,
and kept his faith in God.

They threw stones until he died,
but before he passed away, he said:

"Forgive them, Father,
for they know not what they do."
Some people do not realize
that God's love is real and true.
We need to know this
and believe that God's love is true.

When someone hurts me,
I'll put my faith in you.
You will help me
through my time of need,
and be with me as I say,

"Forgive them, Father,
for they know not what they do."

— *Pamela*

Asking Forgiveness .

God, please help me to ask you for forgiveness when I sin—sooner, not later.

Whenever I do something wrong, my conscience prods me and I feel guilty. Help me not to ignore my guilt, but to desire your wonderful gift of divine forgiveness. Keeping sins shut up inside of me is not good. So help me to take responsibility for the wrong things I have done and not ignore what my conscience tells me. Help me to receive the sacrament of Reconciliation and cleanse me from sin. Amen.

— *Rob*

SELF-CONFIDENCE

I'm Unique

Dear God, please forgive me for not being true to myself. Sometimes I act like someone else and try to imitate others. But I know I shouldn't, because you made me different from everyone else. You made me a unique individual, not a mimic of some other person. I'm thankful you created me and I'll try to live my life in a way that gives glory to you. I love you dearly, Lord, with all my heart. Amen.

— *Nikki*

Self-Doubt

Dear Protector,
sometimes I think negatively about myself,
and say that I can't do something.
Sorry for doubting myself, Lord,
'cause I know I'm one of your creations,
whom you watch over and love and guide.
Please forgive me for thinking
I'm not capable of accomplishing something,
because I know that with your help,
anything is possible.

— *Bree*

Accepting My Body

Dear God, please forgive me for not appreciating the body that you gave me. Sometimes I don't like myself, the person you made me to be, and I wish that I was skinnier or better looking. Please forgive me for hating my appearance and wishing I looked different. Forgive me when I feel jealous and sad that I don't look like someone else. Help me to understand that what is really important is how I take care of the body you gave me. Guide me to accept myself as I am and to focus on more than just my appearance.

— *Barb*

Being Myself

Dear God, please help me to be myself. Sometimes I act differently when I'm around others. I'm not exactly sure why; maybe I'm just trying to show off or act cool. Don't ever let me forget that if you wanted me to be different, you would have made me that way. Please help me be myself around others. I like the way you made me and I want everyone to know the real me.

— *Lori*

True Beauty

Father, you've created me in your beautiful image and likeness. In my heart, I know you love me, but I'm constantly confronted with the picture that society paints as beautiful. Help me to realize that you truly know each hair on my head, each gleam of light in my eyes, and every wrinkle when I smile.

You mold me as a potter shapes a piece of clay, perfecting each part with your loving hands. I'm the child you envisioned I would be. I am perfect in your eyes, and each day you look upon me in love. Let me always remember that you've created me uniquely and beautifully. Help me to see you each day when I look in the mirror, and to realize that physical beauty is so small in comparison to the beauty of *who I am*. Amen.

— *Joan*

A Dating Break

Lord, I appreciate my relationship with family and friends, but lately, I feel kind of obsessed about finding "that special someone." I'm always searching for a special relationship, someone to go out with on the weekend, someone to call every night.

Lord, help me to know that it's okay not to be dating right now. It's hard to feel like I'm alone when everyone else "has someone," but help me to feel secure in who I am. Help me to grow closer to you, Lord, and to enjoy the good things in my life. Thank you, Lord. Amen.

— *Daisy*

Courage to Do Right

Jesus, please help me not to get caught up in trying to please everyone and be popular. I know that this isn't important in the end, and I need to work on pleasing you. Give me the courage to speak up when my friends want me to do something wrong. Help me not to make fun of others or just go along with it when one of my friends does something cruel to somebody. Please give me a loving heart, and help me to find the good in everyone. Lord, I need the strength to encourage my friends in the right way or walk away if they continue down the wrong path. Please walk by my side and guard me from evil. Amen.

— *Ann Marie*

God Loves the Real Me

Lord,
you love me.
Not only the good me,
but the me I'm sometimes ashamed of.
With all my faults,
all my pettiness,
sins, and
weaknesses,
you love me.

For myself.
Not who I could be,
not who I want to be,
not who I try to be—
but who I am.
It's hard to believe
that someone could do that,
just love everything about me,

while encouraging me to change
the mean and small things
about myself.
Thank you for always
loving me. Amen.

— *Jason*

Fighting This Eating Disorder

My God,

I know I can't do anything without you.

I know I'm weak.

I need you.

I explain to others how anorexia feels,

but you already know.

You know me so well.

Continue to give me the strength to fight this
    battle,

and to ask for help when I need it.

In the long hours of the day when I feel lonely or
    sad,

be with me.

Help me to run to you,

give me the grace to continue on.

Let me remember today how much you love and
    care for me.

— *Erin*

Struggling for Inner Beauty

Dear Lord, help me to know that I am your beloved, created in your image. Help me to realize that you created me to be *me*, and no one else, and that I am irreplaceable and wonderful in your eyes.

Your fingers fashioned me in my mother's womb: I am your treasure. Help me to see that beauty is something that you have placed within me. It's not something that I can put on or take off. I have to uncover it.

Help me to know that my worth isn't based on what anyone thinks of me. Help me to believe that I have dignity, as your precious child, forever. And help me to always see the dignity in others, too. Amen.

— *Melissa*

No One Knows Me

Are you there, Lord?
I feel so alone.
It's like no one knows the real me,
and if they did, they wouldn't like me.
Help me to believe and trust in you.
Please, Lord,
walk with me and protect me from evil.
Help me to see the good in others
and myself
and know you are with me. Amen.

— *Jack*

PEER PRESSURE

Trying to Fit In

Lord, I've tried it all. I've tried to be someone I'm not, just so I could be popular. I'm sorry if this insults you, my Creator…but sometimes it's hard to believe I'm really loved. Do you love me just as I am, without the makeup and the cool clothes? I can't believe that anyone could ever love me this way. But the Bible says you do: you love me even with all of my faults!

Lord, help me to see myself the way you see me. Help me to see that I'm worthy of love. Open the eyes of my heart, Lord. Help me to see you as you are: loving me for who I am. Hold me close to your heart and don't let me ever forget your love for me. You gave your life for me. What an act of supreme love! Thank you! Stay close to me, Lord. Be with me always. Amen.

— *Corin*

Mistakes

Dear Jesus, please forgive me for all I've done wrong, for all the people I've hurt with my words and my actions. Help me to think about what you would do in my place. Many times I go along with a group of friends and do something I shouldn't be doing, just so they'll like me. Sometimes I laugh at someone who makes a mistake, even though I know I make thousands of mistakes and I hate it when people make fun of me. Help me to stand up to my peers and do what is right. You created me to do good things, but many times I fail to do so because I'm so caught up with my own life and with stuff that isn't even important. Forgive me please. Help me to learn from my mistakes and not repeat them. The next time I'm faced with a difficult decision between right and wrong, guide me to do what you would want me to do. Amen.

— *Melissa*

Choosing to Do Right

Lord, I'm asking you for the courage to do what
    is right.
Please help me to try to be faithful.
I want to learn to be more like you,
to follow your example of goodness.
If I can do what is right,
maybe I can help others to find the strength to
    do it, too.
Help me to resist the pressure to do something
    wrong,
especially if everyone else is doing it.
Please, God, I ask you for strength
to always make good and wise decisions. Amen.

— *Breanna*

Cheap Thrills

Lord,
I'm so torn.
I want to be popular.
I want to be cool.
I sometimes do things to make myself look good
or so that the popular crowd will notice me.
I laugh and make fun of others just for a few
     cheap laughs.
Give me the courage to turn away from cheap
     thrills
and to be strong enough to choose what I know
     is right. Amen.

— *Karen*

Help Me to Stop Drinking

Father,

I find myself doing the wrong thing:

give me your prudence.

The things I do not want to face make me weak:

give me your strength.

I fear my friends will hate me if I stop:

give me your courage.

Drinking has taken over my life:

bring me back to you.

Alcohol clouds my judgment:

give me your guidance.

It brings me further into sin:

make me pure of heart.

Father, you and only you can help me.

I understand that without you I am weak.

I need you to guide my actions and my words.

I am lost, Lord, bring me home.

— Jan

Struggling with Addiction

Dear God, help me—I've lost my way! Somehow, I've taken up with something wrong. I've tried to get out of this dark place, but I can't do it by myself. I know I'm hurting everyone—Mom and Dad and all of my family. I'm hurting myself, too, but I just can't stop.

Jesus, please don't give up on me. You said, "I am the way." Help me to get back on the right path. I'm so scared; don't leave me alone.

Mary, hold my hand and keep picking me up. Lead me back to your Son. Help me get past these messed-up desires, the voices that tell me I'll never be okay again.

I want to stop. I just can't do it alone.

—Jo

FAMILY

Blessings of Family

Thank you, Father, for all the blessings you have
  given my family.

Thank you for keeping us healthy.

Thank you for our home, our food, and our
  schools.

Thank you for the time we spend together.

Help us to forgive one another when we fight
and talk to each other when we're mad.

Help us to do the right thing.

Guide us as we try to live as your followers. Amen.

— *Tony*

Struggling with My Parents

Please help me, God. I'm having trouble with my mom and dad. They tell me to do something …and sometimes I do it. But a lot of times I don't. Then they get crabby and yell at me, and I get mad and yell back. Help me just to do what they ask, when they ask me to. I know I need your help because sometimes it's just hard. Amen.

— *Marv*

Living Through Divorce

Help me shut out the sounds of my parents' fighting. They're breaking up my home—I feel like my whole life is falling in around me and I can't stand it! Please help me not to take sides and to forgive them for this enormous hurt. Let me love them both and see the good in both of them.

I know that you're always with me and you love me. I know Mary is near to comfort me, and I know your angels surround me to protect me. The problem is that I can't see you, and the people I *can* see are tearing my life apart. Help me, God, help me Amen.

—Jo

Hard Times

God, please help me to get along with my family. It seems like I'm always messing up. I know that when they criticize me they are trying to motivate me to do better, but it still hurts. Help me to look for the good in them and to learn to think before I get angry and say awful things. When I fail, help me to say I am sorry. Please help me in difficult situations and show me how to offer others respect and love. Amen.

— *Justin*

Help Us Get Along

Lord, I had another fight with Mom. Please help us to get along. Forgive me for the awful things I said, and give me the strength to ask her for forgiveness, too. I don't really want to, but I know it's the right thing to do. I know she loves me, but sometimes I don't understand her ways. Enlighten us both, Lord. Amen.

— *Corin*

Younger Siblings

Dear God,
please forgive me for yelling at my siblings.
Help me to let them know I care.
Help me to become a better role model.
When they make mistakes,
let me explain things patiently.
If they ask me to play with them,
let me make the time
or explain why I can't *nicely.*
When my parents ask me to baby-sit,
help me to do so gladly,
without asking for money.
Help me to value time with my family,
and to treasure it forever. Amen.

— *Emily*

Worried about Dad

Dear God, Dad's been really quiet lately, and I'm afraid something's wrong. He went to the doctor last week and seemed preoccupied when he came home. When I asked about it, he said everything was fine, but I don't believe it. What if he's sick? What if he's got cancer or something else? I'm scared, God, and I just want things to be okay. Help us to get through this, and help me to find a way to talk to him. Thanks for listening.

— Jack

Mixed Blessings

Sometimes my family is cool. When my step-brother and I get along, there's always someone to hang around with.

Sometimes my family is a pain. It's hard letting "outsiders" in and seeing them get extra attention.

Sometimes it gets crazy, and I just want to go to my room and slam the door, but then I remember it's not just *my* room anymore...it's his, too! I just want things to be like they were before. Is that so wrong? But I also want this new family to work.

Be with me, God. I could use a friend. Amen.

— *Greg*

PRAYERS OF THANKS

Night Prayer

Dear Lord,
thank you for this day.
Each day you teach me more and more,
and today was no exception.
Let me fall asleep now
without worries and anxiety,
so I will be ready for another day,
and spend tomorrow learning, as I spent today.
Amen.

— *Aaron*

Thank You, God, for Everything

Thank you, God, for everything, the BIG things
    and the small.
For every good gift comes from you, the giver of
    them all.
And all too often I accept, without any thanks
    or praise,
the gifts you send as blessings each day in many
    ways.
I thank you for the little things that often come
    my way,
the things I take for granted and don't mention
    when I pray.
I thank you for the miracles I am much too blind
    to see.
Give me more awareness of my many gifts from
    thee.

And help me to remember that the key to life
    and living
is to make each prayer a prayer of thanks and
    every day thanksgiving. Amen.

                    — *Michael*

Help Me to Be Optimistic

Dear Holy One,
thank you for creating me and loving me.
Because I'm grateful for the gifts you've given me,
I'll try to do my best in everything, with your help.
From now on, I'll turn negatives into positives,
and I will try to see my problems as opportunities to love you more.
Lord, from this day forward,
I'll do my best to show everyone
that I'm created in your image and likeness.

— *Camilla*

The Wonders of Creation

Dear God, thank you for the amazing world you've made. From rocky mountain peaks to oceans and lakes, you made the earth beautiful and fruitful to meet our needs. From the beautiful sky to the rich soil, your creation is glorious. I especially thank you this day for (*mention what you're thankful for*).

Help me, Lord, to preserve the wonders of your world. Let nature remind me especially of your love for us, your children. When I look at the beauty of creation, may it remind me of the beauty of your heavenly Kingdom. Amen.

— *Christopher*

For Life

Father, I'm so happy that you gave me a chance to live. Help me to use my life to glorify you and to make the world a better place. I feel so thankful just to be alive today! What an awesome feeling.

— *Kristen*

Thanks for Being My Rock

Lord, thanks for being my Rock, something solid that won't change. My life can be so unpredictable and confusing; sometimes I don't feel like I have anyone I can really trust! Thank you for always being there. Without you, I could never handle all the curve balls life throws me.

— *Bobby*

For Being There

Dear Lord, thank you for always being there. When things get rough, I know that I can talk to you. If something embarrassing happens and I don't feel like talking about it with my friends or parents, you're there to hear me out. I know you won't laugh at me or think differently of me. When I feel sad and angry, I can tell you and I know that you'll understand. When I tell you my good news, I know that you are happy for me. You're always ready to listen to me even though I sometimes don't listen to you. Thank you for letting me talk to you freely. Thank you for always being there, Lord.

— *Brianna*

For This Day

O mighty Creator of the heavens and earth,
I want to thank you for the good day I've had
     today,
full of praise, grace, and blessings.
I like to remember as I look at the stars
that you created them with love and care,
just as you created me.
And just like the stars, we're all special and
     beautiful
in our own unique way…and we honor you
     when we let it show!
This good day was made by you,
and I thank you for being with me
every step of the way today,
supporting me with your love and care.
Tomorrow, may I bless the good that cheers me up
and use the bad moments to become stronger.

— *Camilla*

PRAYERS TO MARY

Prayer to My Mother

Mother Mary, I do not know what I need, but you do.

You know what I need to grow in faith, in hope, and in love.

You know what I need to grow closer to Jesus.

I offer my prayers to you that you may take them to your Son.

Thank you for your commitment to me, Mary.

Mother of Jesus, please hear my prayer. Amen.

— *Marianne*

Be With Me, Mary

Dear Mary, my Mother, please comfort me when I am suffering. Please stay by my side when I am confronted with trouble. Please guide me to choose what is good and be ever at my side. Amen.

— *Megan*

A Plea to Mary

Mary, help me to be a genuine, gentle person who seeks to love the Father and to follow the Son, in the grace of the Spirit. Amen.

— *Carrie*

A Teen's Prayer to Mary

Dear Mary,
please help me to be respectful and kind toward others.
Help me to be prudent and wise in all situations.
Please lead me every day.
Most of all, guide me to your Son, Jesus. Amen
— *Alexia*

Help Me to Trust God

Dear Mother, when the angel came to you, you said yes with complete trust. Help me to do as you did and say yes with complete trust and love when asked to choose the way of God. Amen.
— *Catherine*

PART II:
TEEN PRAYERS
TO THE SAINTS

PART II: TEEN PRAYERS TO THE SAINTS

We can learn so much by looking at the lives of the saints. *The Catechism of the Catholic Church* tells us: "The witnesses who have preceded us into the kingdom, especially those whom the Church recognizes as saints, share in the living tradition of prayer by the example of their lives, the transmission of their writings, and their prayer today. They contemplate God, praise him, and constantly care for those whom they have left on earth" (no. 2683). We often ask a friend to pray or intercede for us. It makes sense to ask the saints to intercede for us with the Lord. Here are some of our favorite saints and our own prayers for their intercession.

St. Francis of Assisi (1182~1226)

St. Francis was a man who was born into a very rich family in Italy. When he was a young man, he was caught up in all these riches until he was called by God to live in poverty and help the poor. St. Francis rebuilt churches, wrote prayers of peace, and glorified God's creation. God spoke to St. Francis in many ways and he reminds us to listen to God's call and do what God asks.

— *Christina*

Prayer

St. Francis, we beg your intercession for peace in the world. We ask that you help us to be instruments of peace and to have respect for others as you did. Help us to value being a good person and helping others more than having the coolest things or the latest gadgets. May we listen to God's call, as you did, and build up the world around us. We ask this through Christ our Lord. Amen.

St. Faustina (1905~1938)

St. Faustina shows us what it means to have compassion for others. She was blessed by God with a special sympathy for those who suffered, and she tried to help others carry their crosses. Jesus made his message of Divine Mercy known through this humble nun from Poland.

— *Therese*

Prayer

Jesus, who offered your friend, St. Faustina, a profound experience of your boundless mercy, grant me, through her intercession, the grace to welcome your mercy in my life and to offer mercy to others.

Although I have not always shown mercy to those in need, let me learn from St. Faustina's spirit of self-sacrifice and virtue. With trusting confidence, I present my petition to you (*mention it here*) through her intercession.

St. Faustina, pray for us!

St. Clare (1193~1253)

St. Clare was born and lived in Assisi, Italy. When Clare was eighteen, she heard St. Francis speak. His message about living according to the Gospel of Jesus was so remarkable that Clare decided she, too, would follow Jesus. She met Francis in a little chapel outside of town, had her hair cut off, and received a poor garment to wear. Thus, Clare became the first of the "Poor Ladies," whom we know today as the Poor Clares. She dedicated her life to prayer, poverty, and joy, and attracted many women to follow her example. Today, women still follow Christ as Poor Clare Nuns.

Sam

Prayer

Lord, please help me see the inner beauty in others, like I see in St. Clare. Teach me to care about what is on the inside, instead of what people look like. Provide me with the faith I need to serve others and to live simply. I ask this in Jesus' name. Amen.

Bl. James Alberione (1884~1971)

James Alberione was born to a very poor family in Italy. He wanted to be a priest and entered the seminary—but was thrown out a few years later because of the books he was reading. He was admitted to another seminary and, on New Year's Eve, 1900, spent four hours in prayer before the Eucharist. During that time, he heard Jesus' invitation to serve him in a special way. This invitation became his guiding light, and Fr. Alberione decided to use the media of communications to spread the Gospel message to as many people as possible. Today, his followers are "apostles of the media," using books, magazines, CDs, DVDs, TV, movies, radio, and the internet to tell the world about Jesus Christ.

— Alison

Prayer

Lord God, the media fill our lives: I can't imagine a day without TV, music, movies, and e-mailing friends! Thank you for giving us Bl. James Alberione as an apostle of the media to show us how media can be used to serve and glorify you and to spread the Good News about Jesus. Inspire me to make good media choices and to look for signs of your presence when I enjoy media with friends and family. I ask this through Jesus Christ, our Lord. Amen.

St. Thérèse of Lisieux (1873~1897)

Are you ever discouraged by the thought of having to do great things and meeting the standards set by others? If so, St. Thérèse of Lisieux is your saint! She believed that each of us can serve God by doing our small, daily tasks with great love. Her "Little Way" to holiness shows us how everyone can become a saint. St. Thérèse of Lisieux, who became a Carmelite nun at age fifteen, could also become easily discouraged, but she learned to trust in Jesus when she felt worried. She can help us do the same.

— *Katie*

Prayer

Saint Thérèse, you were so close to Jesus. Please show me how to take everything I do and every word I say today and offer it to him. Help me to get right back up when I fall and to never give in to discouragement or anxiety, no matter how many times things go wrong. You always trusted in Jesus' love for you and constantly showed your love in return. Please intercede for me, so that I may share your simple, hopeful, and caring example in my everyday life. Amen.

St. Pio of Pietrelcina (1887~1968)

Padre Pio of Pietrelcina was born in a small village in Italy in 1887. When he was sixteen years old, he joined the Franciscan Order and became a priest. In 1918, during a vision, he mysteriously received the five wounds of Christ, called the stigmata. Although he had these wounds for the rest of his life, Padre Pio considered them secondary to the more important duty of living a good Christian life. Padre Pio treated everyone with fairness and respect, living his faith to the fullest. He died in 1968 and was proclaimed a saint in 2002.

— *Alex*

Prayer

St. Pio, help me to love the Lord and to be strong. In my difficult times, increase my faith so I can love and serve God like you did, by treating everyone with great respect. Christ offered you his wounds as a mysterious sign of love. Please pray that I, too, may be blessed with an intimate relationship with Jesus. Amen.

Bl. Teresa of Calcutta (1910~1997)

Mother Teresa of Calcutta, foundress of the Missionaries of Charity, was a humble sister with a burning desire to serve the "poorest of the poor." She began by taking care of the dying in Calcutta, India, and from there, reached out to the rest of the world's sick, homeless, and unwanted. She believed that Jesus was especially present in the poor, and that serving him in them was to do "something beautiful for God." She received the Nobel Peace Prize in 1979 and became one of the most recognizable Catholic figures of the twentieth century. She was beatified in 2003.

— Thuy

Prayer

Jesus, help me to recognize you in the poor and those with any kind of need. Help me to be generous not only with material things, but especially with my time. As did your friend, Mother Teresa, may I serve you by doing "something beautiful for God" with my life. Amen.

St. Juan Diego (sixteenth century)

In 1531, a Mexican Indian named Juan Diego was on his way to Mass one day, when he passed by a hill at Tepeyac—near today's Mexico City—and saw a beautiful young woman. She told him that a church should be built on that spot. Juan went to tell the bishop, who didn't believe him. The Lady, who said she was the Mother of God, sent him back to the bishop several times, the final time with roses hidden in his cloak as proof. When he opened his cloak, the roses fell to the floor and an image of Our Lady appeared on the cloak. The image of Mary is still visible on Juan's cloak today.

— José

Prayer

Lord God, through your Mother, you called your humble servant, Juan Diego, to a task that seemed too great for him at first. Even though he was not successful at first, Juan persevered in doing what Mary asked, and many people came to know about you because of it. Give me steadfastness and courage in doing what is right and in serving you and your Mother. Through Christ, our Lord. Amen.

St. Bakhita (1869~1947)

Bakhita was a young girl from the African country of Sudan. In 1878, when she was nine years old, Bakhita was kidnapped from her village and turned into a slave. It was several years before she was taken to Italy, where slavery was illegal, and freed. In Italy, Bakhita heard the Gospel message and was baptized. She joined the Daughters of Charity and performed simple tasks such as sewing, cooking, and answering the convent door. She lived a very ordinary life, but her prayer life was extraordinary. She died in 1947, and in 2000, she became the first native of the Sudan to be canonized.

— *Kari*

Prayer

Dear Lord, your friend, Bakhita, suffered greatly during her life, yet she did not seek revenge on those who had hurt her. Instead, she chose to forgive and to use her energies in serving you. Just as she found you in the small, ordinary tasks of life, I, too, want to find you among the daily events of my life: school, homework, church, activities, family life. Please help me to choose love rather than hatred, forgiveness rather than revenge, and kindness rather than meanness. Amen.

Bl. Pier Giorgio Frassati (1901~1925)

Bl. Pier Giorgio Frassati was a young man with a true love for Christ. He was born in 1901 into a rich family in Turin, Italy. A great practical joker, Pier Giorgio was popular and had many friends. He shared his faith with his friends while they camped and hiked together. He went to Mass daily and spent time in prayer each day. He frequently gave his allowance and train fare to the poor. When his father asked Pier Giorgio if he wanted his graduation present to be a new car or money, Pier Giorgio asked for the money—and gave it to a poor family. He worked with the needy and the sick. Bl. Pier Giorgio contracted polio and died when he was just twenty-four years old.

— *Danny*

Prayer

Thank you, Lord, for giving us Bl. Pier Giorgio Frassati as a good example of how fun, friends, and God can go together. Help me to be more like him. Give me opportunities to bring comfort to the poor, the sick, and the dying. Give me the courage to share my faith with my friends. With the help of Bl. Pier Giorgio, help me to know and love you more each day. Amen.

St. Katharine Drexel (1858~1955)

Katharine Drexel was the daughter of a millionaire banker in Philadelphia, Pennsylvania. Shortly after Katharine was born, her mother died, and she was raised by her father and a kind stepmother. Katharine decided to give her life to serving the needs of the poor. She started the Sisters of the Blessed Sacrament and was very dedicated to the Eucharist. The group worked to share the Catholic faith as they served the needs of Native and African Americans. St. Katharine used her family's fortune to help others and to start many schools.

— Jessica

Prayer

St. Katharine, you gave your life in service and used your blessings to help others. Please help me to be aware of the poor and needy around me, and to do my best to support them. Increase my love for Jesus in the Eucharist and inspire my actions so I can lead others to God. Amen.

St. Vincent de Paul (1580~1660)

St. Vincent de Paul is a great saint who lived about 300 years ago. He was a holy man who was sold into slavery shortly after his ordination to the priesthood. He was later freed and returned to his native France where he devoted himself to serving the poor, sick, and needy. He constantly tried to bring the word of God to the poor people he helped. Today, many organizations around the world bear his name and carry out his work.

— Vince

Prayer

St. Vincent, help me to remember those in need. Remind me of the sick, of the poor, of the needy all around the world. Help me to be more like you by being eager to assist those in need—no matter who they are or where they come from—in whatever small way I can. I will try not to take for granted the food I eat, the home I live in, and the clothes I wear. I will try to be more like you, St. Vincent, and help everyone with loving care. Amen.

St. John Bosco (1815~1888)

John Bosco was born in 1815 in Turin, Italy. His father died when he was only two years old, and his mother had to work hard to support the family. When John was old enough, he did odd jobs to make money to help his mother. In order to go to school, John worked as a carpenter, a shoemaker, a cook, a tailor, and a farmer. He enjoyed practicing circus tricks and putting on shows for his friends, and after his performances, John would repeat a homily he had heard earlier in church. John loved to share his faith and tell others about God, and he decided to become a priest. After he was ordained, he took in homeless boys and taught them trades so they could support themselves. He also started a religious order called the Salesians.

— *Hannah and Brennan*

Prayer

Lord, through the intercession of St. John Bosco, help me develop my talents and be a good student. Show me how I can use my talents to attract others to you. Help me to dedicate myself to sharing the Gospel and living my life for you. Amen.

St. Paul (first century)

Paul persecuted followers of Jesus in the early Church until Jesus spoke to him one day on the road to Damascus. He heard Jesus' voice, understood that Jesus was the Lord, and became his follower. Paul traveled all over the world preaching the Gospel and gathering together communities of those who believed in Jesus. Paul suffered for his faith: he was whipped, stoned, shipwrecked, and rejected by some of his friends. Still, he found great joy in serving the Lord, and wrote letters that we can read in the New Testament. He introduced countless people to Jesus until he was sentenced to death and beheaded in Rome.

— Molly and Jessica

Prayer

Lord, through the intercession of St. Paul, help me to trust in you. Give me the wisdom to know what you want me to do and the courage to carry it out. Even when suffering comes my way because of my faith, strengthen me to stand up for what I know is right. Bless me with the ability to find joy in my difficulties. Guide me to be more like St. Paul. Amen.

St. Elizabeth Ann Seton (1774~1821)

St. Elizabeth Ann Seton, better known as Mother Seton, was born in New York City into a wealthy Episcopal family. She married William Seton in 1794, and they had five children. When William became sick, they went to Italy for his health, but he died shortly after their arrival. Elizabeth stayed in Florence for a little while and, through the witness of one of her friends, became very interested in the Catholic faith.

When Elizabeth returned to the United States in 1805, she decided to become Catholic. Many people were against her joining the Church, but she knew it was the right thing to do. She eventually founded the Sisters of Charity and started the first Catholic school system in the United States.

— Janessa

Prayer

St. Elizabeth Ann Seton, pray that I may be like you. You became a Catholic because of the good influence of your friend; help me choose friends that will encourage me to be my best self. Remind me to have courage when unexpected things happen, and guide me to live my life in a way that pleases God. Please help me to find good in troubled times. I ask this in the name of our Lord Jesus Christ. Amen.

PART III:
TEENS' FAVORITE
TRADITIONAL PRAYERS

PART III: TEENS' FAVORITE TRADITIONAL PRAYERS

As Catholics, we are blessed with a treasury of prayers that have come down to us through the years. When it's difficult to find our own words to pray, we can use one of the many prayers that have been passed on to us. When we gather together to worship, we can find joy by praying familiar prayers with our family of faith. These beautiful prayers keep us connected to our Catholic beliefs and help us to grow closer to God. Here are some of our favorite traditional prayers.

Sign of the Cross

By naming the three persons of the Trinity and tracing the symbol of the cross on myself, this short prayer helps me proclaim my faith in both words and actions. When I use holy water to make the Sign of the Cross, it reminds me that I'm baptized— and that makes a difference in my life! Making the Sign of the Cross when I feel afraid helps me to remember that God is always with me and that all I do is in his name.

— Enrique

In the name of the Father, of the Son, and of the Holy Spirit. Amen.

The Our Father

When Jesus' friends asked him how to pray, this is the prayer he taught them. You can find it in your Bible: Matthew 6:7~13. It's awesome to think that we have the same Father as Jesus! I try to pray it when I wake up and before I go to sleep, to ask God for the world's many needs.

— *Samona*

Our Father,
who art in heaven,
hallowed be thy name;
Thy kingdom come;
thy will be done on earth as it is in heaven.
Give us this day our daily bread;
and forgive us our trespasses as we forgive those
who trespass against us,
and lead us not into temptation,
but deliver us from evil. Amen.

Hail Mary

I like the Hail Mary because I have a special devotion to the Blessed Mother. This prayer reminds me of how dedicated Mary was to say yes. The Hail Mary makes me feel the Queen of Heaven is praying for me and that Jesus loves me and will never leave me.

— *Alyssa*

Hail Mary, full of grace!

The Lord is with you;

Blessed are you among women,

and blessed is the fruit of your womb, Jesus.

Holy Mary, Mother of God, pray for us sinners,

now and at the hour of our death. Amen.

Glory

This wonderful short prayer is very powerful and meaningful. It is easy to say anywhere and gives praise to the Trinity. I like to say it every day because it reminds me that I will someday enjoy everlasting life.

— Kevin

Glory to the Father, and to the Son, and to the Holy Spirit,

as it was in the beginning, is now, and will be forever. Amen.

The Apostles' Creed

I used to think this was just a really long prayer. Then I learned that Christians have been praying a form of it since the fourth century A.D.! That made me pay more attention to it, and now I realize how important it is to know what all Catholics believe in. Praying it makes me feel united to all the followers of Jesus throughout the ages!

— Brianna

I believe in God, the Father almighty,
    creator of heaven and earth.

I believe in Jesus Christ, his only Son, our Lord.
    He was conceived by the power of the Holy
        Spirit
        and born of the Virgin Mary.
    He suffered under Pontius Pilate,
        was crucified, died, and was buried.
    He descended to the dead.
    On the third day, he rose again.
    He ascended into heaven,
        and is seated at the right hand of the Father.
    He will come to judge the living and the dead.

I believe in the Holy Spirit,
    the holy catholic Church,
    the communion of saints,
    the forgiveness of sins,
    the resurrection of the body,
    and the life everlasting. Amen.

Act of Faith

This prayer reminds me that Jesus lived, died, and rose for me. When I pray it sincerely, the Act of Faith encourages me and I feel happy to be Catholic.

— *Ashley*

O my God, I firmly believe that you are one God in three divine Persons, Father, Son, and Holy Spirit. I believe that your divine Son became man and died for our sins, and that he will come to judge the living and the dead. I believe these and all the truths which the holy Catholic Church teaches, because you revealed them, who can neither deceive nor be deceived. Amen.

Act of Hope

This is a strong, short prayer, and I pray it when I am feeling bad about something in my life. By dying on the cross, Jesus made the ultimate sacrifice and showed how much God loves me and all people. I always feel better after asking God to fill me with his grace.

— *Lauren*

O my God, relying on your almighty power and infinite goodness and promises, I hope to obtain pardon of my sins, the help of your grace, and life everlasting, through the merits of Jesus Christ, my Lord and Redeemer. Amen.

Act of Love

This prayer helps me to forgive others and ask for forgiveness from everyone I have hurt. It makes me focus on my relationship with God and realize that I need to give my best to God. It helps me feel I can turn to God for anything.

—Kelsey

O my God, I love you above all things, with my whole heart and soul, because you are all-good and worthy of all love. I love my neighbor as myself for the love of you. I forgive all who have injured me, and I ask pardon of all whom I have injured.

Act of Contrition

I like the Act of Contrition because it tells God how sorry I am for the times I have sinned. I say the Act of Contrition when I go to confession and at the end of each day. This prayer reminds me that there is hope in the world and that God is merciful. I always feel better after saying the Act of Contrition.

— *Max*

My God,
I am sorry for my sins with all my heart.
In choosing to do wrong
and failing to do good,
I have sinned against you
whom I should love above all things.
I firmly intend, with your help,
to do penance,
to sin no more,
and to avoid whatever leads me to sin.

Our Savior Jesus Christ
suffered and died for us.
In his name, my God, have mercy. Amen.

Angelus

This is a special prayer that honors the "yes" Mary said to God when she was asked to be the Mother of Jesus. You can read about this event, called the Annunciation, in Luke's Gospel (1:26–38). Sometimes I need help saying "yes" to God, and I pray this prayer to ask Mary to guide me.

— *Kevin*

V. The angel spoke God's message to Mary,

R. and she conceived of the Holy Spirit.

Hail, Mary.

V. "I am the lowly servant of the Lord:

R. Let it be done to me according to your word."

Hail, Mary.

V. And the Word became flesh

R. and lived among us.

Hail, Mary.

V. Pray for us, Holy Mother of God,
R. that we may become worthy of the promises
of Christ.

Let us pray.

Lord,
fill our hearts with your grace:
once, through the message of an angel
you revealed to us the incarnation of your Son;
now, through his suffering and death
lead us to the glory of his resurrection.
We ask this through Christ our Lord.

R. Amen.

The Divine Praises

I love this prayer because it reveals the awesomeness of God. I usually say this prayer during Eucharistic adoration or I read it when I wake up in the morning. The Divine Praises prayer gives me a chance to think about the greatness of God.

— *Victoria*

Blessed be God.

Blessed be his Holy Name.

Blessed be Jesus Christ, true God and true Man.

Blessed be the name of Jesus.

Blessed be his most Sacred Heart.

Blessed be his most Precious Blood.

Blessed be Jesus in the most holy Sacrament of the Altar.

Blessed be the Holy Spirit, the Paraclete.

Blessed be the great Mother of God, Mary most holy.

Blessed be her holy and Immaculate Conception.

Blessed be her glorious Assumption.

Blessed be the name of Mary, Virgin and Mother.

Blessed be St. Joseph, her most chaste spouse.

Blessed be God in his angels and in his saints.

Anima Christi

The Anima Christi *is one of my favorite prayers and reminds me that I find nourishment in Jesus Christ. "Anima Christi" means "Soul of Christ." This prayer expresses my need and longing for Christ because I am nothing without him.*

— *Victoria*

Soul of Christ, sanctify me.
Body of Christ, heal me.
Blood of Christ, drench me.
Water from the side of Christ, wash me.
Passion of Christ, strengthen me.

Good Jesus, hear me.

In your wounds shelter me.
From turning away keep me.
From the evil one protect me.
At the hour of my death call me.
Into your presence lead me,
to praise you with all your saints
for ever and ever.
Amen.

Peace Prayer of St. Francis

Peace is so important, but it's hard to find and even harder to keep. I have a card with this prayer in my Bible and pray it every night. I pray for peace in the world and for my family and friends.

— *Tanya*

Lord,

make me an instrument of your peace.

Where there is hatred let me sow love;

where there is injury, pardon;

where there is doubt, faith;

where there is despair, hope;

where there is darkness, light;

and where there is sadness, joy.

O Divine Master, grant that I may not so much seek to be consoled as to console; to be understood as to understand; to be loved as to love; for it is in giving that we receive, it is in pardoning that we are pardoned, and it is in dying that we are born to eternal life.

Serenity Prayer

I learned this prayer in Alateen, a support group for teens who have an alcoholic in their family. In tough times, it helps me remember that I can only live one day at a time, and that the wisdom for living a good life comes as a gift of the Holy Spirit.
— *Jeanne*

God, grant me the serenity to accept the things I can't change, courage to change the things I can, and wisdom to know the difference.

St. Patrick's Breastplate

This prayer is attributed to St. Patrick, who brought Christianity to Ireland in the fifth century. I love thinking that Christ surrounds me and protects me like a suit of armor, only better! It reminds me that Jesus is with me no matter where I am or who I'm with. Praying this prayer makes me want to be a better person and to respect Christ, who is always near.

— Colin

Christ with me, Christ before me,
Christ behind me, Christ within me,
Christ under me, Christ above me,
Christ at my right, Christ at my left,
Christ in lying down, Christ in sitting, Christ in
      rising up.
Christ in the heart of everyone who thinks of me,
Christ in the mouth of everyone who speaks to me,
Christ in every eye that sees me,
Christ in every ear that hears me.

Don't Quit

We have a card with this prayer on our refrigerator. My dad hung it there during a really rough time our family had, and we got through it. Every time I go into the kitchen, I read the first few lines. It encourages me not to give up, but to keep praying and to keep trying to do my best.

— *Marc*

When things go wrong as they sometimes will.
When the road you're trudging seems all up-hill.
When funds are low and the debts are high.
And you want to smile, but you have to sigh.
When care is pressing you down a bit.
Rest, if you must, but don't you quit.

Life is strange with its twists and turns
as everyone of us sometimes learns.
And many a failure turns about
when he might have won had he stuck it out.
Don't give up though the pace seems slow
you may succeed with another blow.

Success is failure turned inside out,

the silver tint of the clouds of doubt,

and you never can tell how close you are,

it may be near when it seems so far.

So stick to the fight when you're hardest hit.

It's when things seem worst that you must not

quit.

Prayer of Cardinal Newman

When I first read this prayer written by Cardinal Newman, a British Anglican churchman who became a Catholic in 1845, I felt it had been written just for me. I did not realize that I was depending totally on myself in my life, and not on God. The prayer has shown me that, though I have to do my part, I must first allow Christ to "possess my whole being." If I allow him to live through me, then everyone I meet cannot help but see Christ through me.

— Katie

Dear Jesus,

help me to spread your love

everywhere I go.

Flood my heart with your Spirit and life.

Penetrate and possess

my whole being so utterly

that all my life may only be

a radiance of yours.

Shine through me,

and be so in me

that everyone I come in contact with
may feel your presence in me.
Let them look up and see no longer me
but only you, dear Jesus. Amen.

Morning Offering

When I wake up each morning, I say this energetic prayer. I can be pretty lazy in the morning, but this prayer helps me get off to a great start. When I pray it, I prepare myself for the day and ask God to be with me and to help me make good decisions. I also offer all my problems to God. The prayer gives me strength for a new day.

— *Dalton*

O Jesus, through the Immaculate Heart of Mary, I offer you all my prayers, works, joys, and sufferings of this day, for all the intentions of your Sacred Heart, in union with the holy Sacrifice of the Mass throughout the world, in reparation for my sins, for the intentions of all our associates, and for the general intention recommended this month. Amen.

Angel of God

When I am frightened or tempted, I just say the Angel of God prayer. It helps me to remember that someone is always watching over me. It helps me to avoid sin and makes me feel protected and safe.

— *Hank*

Angel of God, my guardian dear,

to whom God's love entrusts me here,

ever this day be at my side,

to light and guard, to rule and guide. Amen.

Prayer Before a Crucifix

This prayer reminds me of how Jesus died on the cross for me and how much he loves me. I like to say this prayer after receiving Jesus in the Eucharist and during Eucharistic adoration.

— *Brendan*

Good and gentle Jesus,
I kneel before you.
I see and I ponder your five wounds.
My eyes behold what was prophesied about you:
"They have pierced my hands and feet;
they have counted all my bones."
Engrave on me this image of yourself.
Fulfill the yearnings of my heart:
give me faith, hope, and love,
repentance for sin,
and true conversion of life. Amen.

Memorare

The word "memorare" is Latin for "remember." This prayer makes me feel close to Mary and helps me know she hears all of my concerns and remembers me when she speaks to her Son.

— *Jamie*

Remember, most loving Virgin Mary,
never was it heard
that anyone who turned to you for help
was left unaided.

Inspired by this confidence,
though burdened by my sins,
I run to your protection
for you are my mother.

Mother of the Word of God,
do not despise my words of pleading
but be merciful and hear my prayer.
Amen.

Hail Holy Queen

I usually say the Hail Holy Queen after I pray the rosary. I like it because it helps me rely on Mary as my mother. This prayer helps me to know that Mary will always be there for me when- ever I need her.

— *Renee*

Hail, holy Queen, Mother of mercy,

Hail, our life, our sweetness, and our hope.

To you we cry, the children of Eve;

to you we send up our sighs,

mourning and weeping in this land of exile.

Turn, then, most gracious advocate,

your eyes of mercy toward us;

lead us home at last

and show unto us the blessed fruit of your womb,

    Jesus:

O clement, O loving, O sweet Virgin Mary.

A Teen's Prayer to Mary and Joseph

I like to pray this prayer before I go on a date, or when I'm in a relationship that's started to become important to me. It reminds me of my values and of what I need to put first in my life.

— *Mary*

Dear Mary, please help me also to be prudent and wise in all situations. Help me be holy and true to myself. Guide me in your way and lead me closer to your Son, Jesus, every day.

Dear Joseph, I ask you to watch over me and my date. Make us strong if we are tempted, and keep us faithful to God, as you were during your life. Amen.

The Divine Mercy Chaplet

Our world has changed dramatically in the past few years, and I think we teens feel especially worried about the world situation because it seems like there is nothing we can really do to help, yet we are old enough to understand the seriousness of what goes on.

The Divine Mercy Chaplet, given by Jesus to St. Faustina in 1935, celebrates the power of God's mercy. This prayer has really pulled me through trying times. It doesn't take long to pray, and it makes me feel that I am doing my part to help the world. If everyone said this Chaplet, imagine how powerful our prayers for peace would be!

— *Mallory*

Use a Rosary to pray this prayer.

Say the Our Father, a Hail Mary, and the Apostles' Creed on the three beads closest to the crucifix.

On the large bead of each decade say: "Eternal Father, I offer you the Body and Blood, Soul and Divinity of our Lord Jesus Christ in atonement for our sins and those of the whole world."

On the ten small beads of each decade say: "For the sake of his sorrowful passion, have mercy on us and on the whole world."

When all five decades are complete, conclude with: "Holy God, Holy Mighty One, Holy Immortal One, have mercy on us and on the whole world" (3 times).

To end the chaplet say: "Jesus, I trust in you."

The Rosary

The Rosary is a Gospel prayer that helps us to pray with Mary so that we can grow closer to her Son, Jesus. Repeating the prayers of the Rosary becomes like gentle background music for the heart of the Rosary, which is meditation on the mysteries of Jesus' life.

The Joyful Mysteries

1. The Annunciation to the Blessed Virgin Mary (Lk 1:38)

2. Mary Visits Her Cousin Elizabeth (Lk 1:45)

3. The Birth of Jesus at Bethlehem (Lk 2:7)

4. The Presentation of Jesus in the Temple (Lk 2:22)

5. The Finding of the Child Jesus in the Temple (Lk 2:49)

The Mysteries of Light

1. John Baptizes Jesus in the Jordan (Mt 3:17)

2. Jesus Reveals His Glory at the Wedding of Cana (Jn 2:5)

3. Jesus Proclaims the Kingdom of God and Calls Us to Conversion (Mk 1:15)

4. The Transfiguration of Jesus (Lk 9:35)

5. Jesus Gives Us the Eucharist (Mk 14:22-24)

The Sorrowful Mysteries

1. Jesus Prays in the Garden of Gethsemane (Lk 22:44)

2. Jesus Is Scourged at the Pillar (Jn 19:1)

3. Jesus Is Crowned with Thorns (Mk 15:17)

4. Jesus Carries the Cross to Calvary (Jn 19:17)

5. Jesus Dies for Our Sins (Jn 19:30)

The Glorious Mysteries

1. Jesus Rises from the Dead (Jn 20:19)

2. Jesus Ascends into Heaven (Mk 16:19)

3. The Holy Spirit Descends on the Apostles (Acts 2:4)

4. Mary Is Assumed into Heaven (Lk 1:48–49)

5. Mary Is Crowned Queen of Heaven and Earth

   (2 Tim 2:12)

Stations of the Cross

"…Jesus said, 'If any want to become my follower, let them deny themselves and take up their cross and follow me. For those who want to save their life will lose it and those who lose their life for my sake will find it. For what will it profit them if they gain the whole world but forfeit their life? Or what will they give in return for their life?'" (Mt 16:24)

First Station
Jesus Is Condemned to Death: *He was silent.*

Second Station
Jesus Takes Up His Cross: *He was accepting.*

Third Station
Jesus Falls Under the Weight of the Cross:
He was exhausted.

Fourth Station
Jesus Meets His Mother: *He was sorrowful.*

Fifth Station
Simon Helps Jesus Carry the Cross:
He was grateful.

Sixth Station
Veronica Wipes the Face of Jesus:
He was compassionate.

Seventh Station
Jesus Falls the Second Time: *He was destitute.*

Eighth Station
Jesus Consoles the Women of Jerusalem:
He was sympathetic.

Ninth Station
Jesus Falls the Third Time: *He was crushed.*

Tenth Station
Jesus Is Stripped of His Garments:
He was lonely.

Eleventh Station
Jesus Is Nailed to the Cross: *He was slain.*

Twelfth Station
Jesus Dies on the Cross: *He was loyal.*

Thirteenth Station
Jesus Is Taken Down from the Cross:
He was helpless.

Fourteenth Station
Jesus Is Laid in the Tomb: *He was at rest.*

On the third day, he rose again!

ACKNOWLEDGMENTS

Many people helped prepare this prayer book, especially those who contributed prayers, listed below. In some cases, pen names are used to protect the privacy of the authors. We were not able to use all the material submitted, but we would like to thank each person that contributed in some way.

Elizabeth Alcott; Edward M. Alonzo; Patrick Andera; Ali Baker; Samantha Barrows; Matthew Baudek; Danny Bieshaar; Hank Braun; Hannah Brennan; Matthew Brolsma; Aaron Brugman; Katie Buckmaster; Max Bush; Breanna Butala; Mallory Carl; Andrea Casias; Michael Cepress; Kristen Claeys; Tony Constancio; Joe Cordella; Stephanie Costello; Carolyn Crabtree; Dan Cremons; David Cullen; Catherine Cullen; Eva Maria Damien; Richard Deanda; Elaine Deiorio; Lucero Derek; Tracy Dolan; Sam Dunn; Gretchen Einfeldt; Tami Erickson; Jamie Feeser; Luke Finney; Mary Flaherty; Lauren Froehle; Teresa Gazich; Ted Gelderman; Carrie Grove; Lizzy Hagget; Anne Harig; Victoria Hausmann; Alex Healy; Brianna Healy; Jessie Hennen; Laura Hentges; Vince Hernandez; David Hicks; Mike Hogan; Emily Holstrom; Edward D.J. Hom; Severin Hubka; Matthew Hudson; Alex Jensen; Catherine Jensen; Sarah Johnston; Anne Kelly; Rose Knauss; Tom Kreitzer; Molly Law; Matt Love; Derek Lucero; Alyssa Maccan; Amy Maddox; Kathleen Majewski; Brenna Manion; Jane Margolis; Bobby Marsland; Kristy McNutt; Tony Miller; Bobby Mittet; Therese Moen; Pamela Molitor; Brendan Monahan; Sarah Moran; Amy Nelson; Janessa Nelson; Amanda Noel; Christopher Ortega; Camila Panama; Mark Paolucci; Laura Potter; Nina E. Prevot;

Jillian Quintana; Nicole Racine; Dalton Ramsey; Alex Ritter; Kelsey Roben; Matt Robinson; Christopher Rydberg; Bernadette M. Sacksteder; Lisa Sandahl; Renee Saunders; Sean Scullin; Dana Silva; Mary Soldner; Mary Stachyra; Sarah Steffes; Marianne Stelly; Margaret Stiemke; Megan Stiemke; Kyle Stines; Peter Stur; Michael Ulrey; Ashley VanVeen; Katie L. Visser; Anastasia VonTilius; Carrie Wagner; Marcus Wells; Christina Wells; Jessica Wells; Rachel Wells; Christine Wienke; Adam Williams; Kevin Willman; Briana Young.

A special thank you goes to the groups of young people that spent hours reading and rating the prayers they liked best. I would also like to thank the following schools, youth groups, friends, and family that assisted in any way.

— *Judith H. Cozzens, Director of the Young Writers Workshop*

All Souls School
Community of Christ the Redeemer Youth Group
Mullen High School
NET Ministries
St. Frances Cabrini Youth Bible Study Group
St. Odilia School
Fran Billars
Jack Cozzens
Claudia Munson
Cheryl Prevot
Lily Reardon

CREDITS

Pauline
BOOKS & MEDIA

The Daughters of St. Paul operate book and media centers at the following addresses. Visit, call or write the one nearest you today, or find us on the World Wide Web, www.pauline.org

CALIFORNIA

3908 Sepulveda Blvd, Culver City, CA 90230   310-397-8676

2640 Broadway Street, Redwood City, CA 94063   650-369-4230

5945 Balboa Avenue, San Diego, CA 92111   858-565-9181

FLORIDA

145 S.W. 107th Avenue, Miami, FL 33174   305-559-6715

HAWAII

1143 Bishop Street, Honolulu, HI 96813   808-521-2731

Neighbor Islands call:
1-866-521-2731

ILLINOIS

172 North Michigan Avenue, Chicago, IL 60601   312-346-4228

LOUISIANA

4403 Veterans Memorial Blvd, Metairie, LA 70006   504-887-7631

MASSACHUSETTS

885 Providence Hwy, Dedham, MA 02026   781-326-5385

MISSOURI

9804 Watson Road, St. Louis, MO 63126   314-965-3512

NEW JERSEY

561 U.S. Route 1, Wick Plaza, Edison, NJ 08817   732-572-1200

NEW YORK

150 East 52nd Street, New York, NY 10022   212-754-1110

PENNSYLVANIA

9171-A Roosevelt Blvd, Philadelphia, PA 19114   215-676-9494

SOUTH CAROLINA

243 King Street, Charleston, SC 29401   843-577-0175

TENNESSEE

4811 Poplar Avenue, Memphis, TN 38117   901-761-2987

TEXAS

114 Main Plaza, San Antonio, TX 78205   210-224-8101

VIRGINIA

1025 King Street, Alexandria, VA 22314   703-549-3806

CANADA

3022 Dufferin Street, Toronto, ON M6B 3T5   416-781-9131

¡También somos su fuente para libros,
videos y música en español!